Five Children and It

E. Nesbit

Adapted by Margaret McAllister

Illustrated by Philippe Dupasquier

Contents

CHAPTER I

Wishes!

It was one of those magical days, the beginning of a holiday. That's why the four children were stretching to see out of the carriage windows, looking out for the house where they'd spend the summer. They were London children, used to rows of dull grey houses in dull grey streets, with nowhere to go. The idea of staying in the countryside was wonderful.

Cyril, who was the eldest, was looking forward to exploring. Anthea, who was next, tried to look after the younger ones – Robert who didn't want to be looked after at all, and

Jane, the youngest. Then there was the baby (they called him the Lamb), who needed a great deal of looking after, sometimes too much.

The carriage took them uphill until Mother said, 'Here we are! This house!'

'It's all white!' said Robert. 'It's like a castle!'

'With a huge garden,' said Anthea, 'and roses!'

'And a plum tree!' added Jane.

'Looks good!' said Cyril, and the Lamb said, 'obbly-obble-oop!' Nobody knew what that meant, but he sounded happy.

The children tumbled over each other to get out of the carriage. It was a wonderful garden, with wild, overgrown places, lawns to run and roll on, orchards, and old stables where you could climb into the loft and the hay made you sneeze. On one side of the house was an old chalk quarry,* and on the other, a gravel pit. It was in the gravel pit* that they made the discovery that changed everything. But it didn't start with the gravel pit.

It began like this. Firstly their father had to go away on business, but they were used to that. Then Mother had to go away and they weren't used to that at all. But Granny was ill and needed Mother to look after her. There were people to take care of them – Cook, who looked after the kitchen, and Martha, who did everything else – but they were both very busy. It wasn't the same as having Mother to take them out and think of interesting things to do.

By the middle of the first day they were getting bored. Cyril felt that, being the eldest, he should think of something.

'Let's go to the gravel pit,' he said. 'We can take spades and pretend it's the beach. Father says it was, thousands of years ago.'

They went down the path, carrying the Lamb, to the gravel pit, which was like a giant-sized basin. First they built a sandcastle. Then they set about digging the deepest hole they possibly could. (The Lamb tried eating sand, was disappointed, cried, and went to sleep.)

Further down, the sand was softer and easier to dig, but it was hot work. It soon stopped being fun.

'This is boring,' said Cyril. 'Let's look at that cave over there.' Robert and Jane went with him, but Anthea went on digging.

Sadly the cave wasn't much to explore. By this time Cyril, Robert and Jane were getting thirsty and wishing they'd brought something to drink. Cyril was about to say that they should go home, when a shriek from Anthea sent them all running to her.

'It's alive!' she screamed. 'Help! It'll get away!'

'What have you found?' demanded Robert. 'A rat?'

'Not a snake!' shrieked Jane.

'Oh, let's see!' said Cyril, jumping into the hole. 'I'd love a pet snake!'

'No!' said Anthea. 'It's too big for a rat and too furry for a snake! It's got feet and hands – and it spoke to me!'

'Don't be so silly!' said Robert. He grabbed a spade and started digging again.

'Don't!' cried Anthea. 'You'll hurt it!' She pushed Robert away and scrabbled with her hands. 'Fur! I can feel it!'

'Let me alone!' said a husky voice. Anthea didn't say, 'I told you so!' but she gave Robert a sharp look.

'Please, please come out!' she said into the hole. 'I wish you would!'

'Oh, you wish, do you?' said the voice – and out of the hole wriggled a fat, furry, brown creature, yawning. It was about the size of a large cat, but with arms, legs, feet and hands like a monkey's, long whiskers and pointed ears like a bat's. Its eyes were on stalks, like a snail's horns, or like telescopes, and it could stretch them out or shorten them.

'Can we take it home?' asked Jane.

The creature turned its long stalk eyes to take a good look at her. 'Does she always talk nonsense?' it asked.

'She doesn't mean to,' said Anthea gently. 'We won't hurt you. Don't be afraid.'

'Afraid!' repeated the creature indignantly. 'Me? Don't you know a Psammead* when you see one?'

'A sammy-add?' repeated Anthea. 'What's that?'

'A sand-fairy, in English,' it said crossly. 'But if you knew anything much, you'd know it was Greek.' It spelled it out. 'P - S - A - M - M - E - A - D. Sammyadd. Sand-fairy. Now go away.' It wriggled down into the sand again.

'Please don't go!' cried Robert. 'You're the most amazing thing ever!'

The Psammead seemed to like this. It stopped trying to burrow into the sand.

'How long have you been here?' asked Robert.

'*Ages*,' said the Psammead. 'Thousands of years. Did you come to ask for a megatherium?'*

'A what?' asked all the children at once.

'You don't know about megatheriums?' asked the sand-fairy. 'In the old days, everyone ate them. There were lots of

Psammeads, and we gave wishes. Small boys
would be sent out in the morning to find a
Psammead and wish for a megatherium, ready
to cook. A megatherium was as big as an
elephant, so there was plenty to eat.'

'Wasn't there a lot left over?' said Anthea,
who knew that food shouldn't be wasted.

'Oh no,' said the Psammead. 'Everything
left over turned to stone* at sunset.'

'But why aren't there lots of Psammeads
now?' asked Robert.

The Psammead's head and whiskers drooped. 'It was very sad,' it said.

'The children used to build castles on the beach for us to live in. But they *would* dig moats around them, and that nasty sea would rush in.'

'Wasn't that fun?' asked Cyril.

'Fun!' said the Psammead. 'We are delicate creatures! If we get wet, we catch cold and die! So there were fewer and fewer of us.'

'Did *you* get wet?' asked Robert.

'Once,' said the Psammead with a shudder. 'On the twelfth hair of my top left whisker. I've had trouble with it ever since. I let the sun dry my whisker. Then I dug a hole in the warm, dry sand, and stayed there. The sea went away. And that's that. Goodbye.'

'Please stay!' said the children, and Jane added, 'Can you really give wishes?'

'I just did,' it said. 'You wished I'd come out, and I did.'

'Oh! Please can we have another one?' asked Jane.

'If you must,' it said grumpily. 'But hurry up
about it.'

That was easier said than done. We all *think*
we know what we'd like if we could have
wishes. But now that they had to choose
something, the children couldn't make up
their minds what they wanted.

'Quickly,' said the Psammead.

Then Anthea remembered a wish that she and Jane had often talked about. 'Please,' she said, 'we wish we were as beautiful as the day.'

'What does that mean?' asked Robert.

'Very, very beautiful,' said Jane.

The Psammead stretched out its eyes on their stalks and seemed to hold its breath and puff itself out until it was twice its normal size. Then it sighed and shrank back down again. 'Sorry,' it said. 'I can't quite manage it. I've got to save my strength for the rest of your wishes. If you just had one wish a day, I could do it.'

'Oh yes!' said the children. 'One wish a day would be fine.'

The Psammead stretched its eyes even further and swelled up more than ever.

'I hope it doesn't hurt itself,' said Anthea.

'Or burst,' said Robert. But then the Psammead suddenly let out its breath and collapsed down to its usual size.

'I hope that didn't hurt,' said Anthea.

'Just my whisker,' it said. 'Kind of you to ask.' Quick as a flash, it buried itself in the sand again. The children looked at each other.

Each of them was looking at three astonishingly beautiful faces. It was like looking at strangers. If it hadn't been for their clothes, which were grubby from the gravel pit, they wouldn't have known each other.

CHAPTER 2

Beautiful as the day

'Cyril, you look like a golden-haired angel!' said Anthea. 'It's not like you. I think I liked you better before. And Robert looks sort of Italian, all dark curly hair and big eyes.'

'And you two girls look like models,' said Robert. 'Let's go home. It must be dinner-time.'

'I'll carry the Lamb,' said Anthea. The baby, who had woken up, took one look at her and howled.

'Come to Anthea, darling,' she said. He screamed even louder.

'Come to Cyril,' said Cyril, and tried to pick

him up, but the Lamb fought and kicked.

'He doesn't know who we are!' said Anthea.

'Oh no!' said Cyril. 'We have to win him over! Our own brother!'

It was an hour before the Lamb would let them carry him home, and by that time they all felt hollow with hunger. When they reached the house, Jane was staggering under the Lamb's weight. She was glad to hand him to Martha, who was waiting for them at the door. Martha snatched him from her.

'Who on Earth are you?' she demanded. 'What are you doing with our baby?'

'We're us!' said Robert. 'I'm Robert!'

'And I'm Cyril!' said Cyril. 'Let us in!'

'Please, we know we look different, but...' began Anthea.

'I don't know who you lot are or what you're up to,' snapped Martha. 'But if our children put you up to this, they'll be in trouble. Shoo!' She shut the door in their faces.

The children banged at the door and rang the bell, but it was no good. They wandered away down the lane, hungry, thirsty, and stunningly beautiful.

It was a long afternoon. Three times they tried to get into the house, but no one would let them in. When Robert tried to climb in through a window, Cook emptied a jug of water over his head and said she would call for the police.

'They can't send you to prison for being beautiful,' said Anthea as they walked away.

'Can they send you to prison for being a nuisance?' asked Cyril, and nobody knew. Tired, with nowhere to go, they sat down under a hedge.

'It'll wear off at sunset,' said Jane. 'Then we'll look normal again.'

'But it might not!' cried Anthea. 'We might turn into stone after sunset, like the megatheriums. We never thought of that!' She burst into tears and so did Jane. Robert sniffed and said he wasn't crying, and Cyril bit his lip and looked hard at the ground.

After a long, miserable silence, Cyril said, 'I don't want to scare you, but I think I'm turning to stone. I can't feel my foot.'

'That's because you've been sitting on it,' snapped Anthea. 'It's gone to sleep.'

This turned out to be true, and they were all very cross with Cyril for giving them such a fright.

'I don't think we'll turn into stone,' said Robert. 'Because the Sammy-thing said we could have another wish tomorrow.'

This was some comfort, but they were still desperately hungry and thirsty.

At last, huddled together for comfort, they fell asleep. When Anthea awoke, the sun had set. She pinched herself to see if it hurt, and to her joy, it did.

'It's all right!' she cried. 'We haven't turned to stone! And Cyril, you're all ugly again! We're ordinary!'

'Where do you think you've been?' demanded Martha when they got home. 'We had some very strange children here this afternoon.'

'They were horrible,' said Anthea. 'They stopped us from coming home until now. We only just got away, and we're starving!'

'Well, don't you go near them again,' said Martha, as Cook brought in a supper that looked and smelled delicious.

'We won't!' said Robert. 'We never want to see them again!'

CHAPTER 3

---◆---

Wealth

Next morning, the children wondered if the Psammead was just a dream. But they decided that they couldn't all have had the same dream, so it must be real. And they wanted to go back to the gravel pit to see if it was still there.

It was Martha's day off. She had put on her favourite purple dress and was going to visit her cousins in Rochester. To the children's delight, she had dressed the Lamb in his best clothes too, and was taking him with her to show him off.

'That's them out of the way,' said Cyril.

'Now for the Psammead.'

They went to the gravel pit, but digging for the Psammead took a long time.

'Maybe we did dream it,' said Robert.

'Why don't you say something sensible?' said Cyril crossly.

'Why don't you boys stop arguing!' said Anthea, and they were all very snappy by the time the Psammead's bat ears appeared.

'How is your whisker?' asked Anthea kindly.

'Uncomfortable,' it said, 'but thank you for asking.'

'May we have a little extra wish today?' asked Robert. 'A tiny one?'

'Hmm,' said the Psammead. 'You could always wish for good tempers. I heard you arguing just now.'

'We wish Martha and Cook won't notice the wishes you give us – I mean, are kind enough to give us,' said Anthea.

The Psammead puffed itself out. 'Done,' it said.

'And our proper wish for today is to have wealth – riches – money,' said Robert. 'Lots, please.'

'It won't do you any good,' said the Psammead. 'Gold, or notes?'

'Gold, please!' they all said.

'How much?' it asked. 'This gravel pit full? Then get out of the way, before it buries you.'

They ran to the edge of the gravel pit, turned, and looked down. GOLD! The whole pit shone, filled to the brim with sparkling gold coins. The children gasped, scooping up handfuls of it.

'It'll be gone by sunset, so make the most of it,' said Cyril. 'Let's fill our pockets and go to Rochester for the day.'

They set out for Rochester, their pockets so heavy with gold that they had to leave small heaps of it behind hedges. Even so, they were still immensely rich by the time they reached the main road.

Anthea hired a pony cart to take them into town from a nice man who said the coins were

'spade guineas',* and was happy to take one in payment. This made everyone feel very grown up, and Anthea asked him if she could buy a horse and carriage. He told her to try Billy Peasemarsh's yard.

After that, nothing went right.

Feeling hot and tired they stopped at a shop, and Cyril went in to buy a drink.

'I had to pay with my ordinary money!' he said when he came out. 'The man in the shop said he didn't have change for gold! Seemed to think it was play money.'

If golden guineas were so valuable, why did nobody in Rochester want them? The children went from shop to shop, and no one liked the look of their money. Some said it was foreign. Some said it was old-fashioned and they didn't take it any more. All of them were very suspicious about how four grubby children could have golden guineas.

By the time three different bakers had refused to serve them, they were so hungry that they ran in to a shop, grabbed a dozen buns and dropped a guinea in front of the baker. He chased them out of the shop, but kept the guinea.

'We still haven't bought a horse and carriage,' said Anthea.

Feeling cheered up by the sticky buns, they went to Billy Peasemarsh's stables and asked Billy Peasemarsh himself – a tall, thin man

with a lean face – to sell them a horse and
carriage, please. Billy Peasemarsh found this
very funny and called for his assistant, Willum.

'This lot think they're royalty,' he said.
'They want to buy the whole stables! I bet they
don't have tuppence.'*

'Tuppence!' exclaimed Robert angrily. 'Look
at *this*!'

It really wasn't a good idea to pull a handful
of golden guineas from his pocket. Before they
could make a run for it, Billy Peasemarsh had
locked the doors of the yard and sent Willum
to get the police.

'But it's our money!' insisted Cyril.

'It's true!' said Jane, who looked ready to cry.

'Where'd you get it from, then?' demanded Billy Peasemarsh. Jane said that they got it from a sand-fairy, and Anthea insisted that she was telling the truth. Billy decided that the boys were thieves and the girls were insane. That was what he told the policeman who arrived.

'I'll take them all to the station,' said the officer. 'They'll be charged with illegal possession of the gold.'

The children had never felt so angry and humiliated as they did now, marching under arrest to the police station. In tears of rage, Robert didn't even notice when he bumped into a woman in the street.

'Robert! Children!' she cried. 'Whatever's going on?'

It was Martha, with the Lamb in her arms, on her way home. The policeman told her why the children were under arrest. But Martha didn't believe a word of it.

'Turn out your pockets, boys,' said the
policeman, so they did. Martha, because of
their first wish in the morning, didn't see a
thing. She was very cross with the policeman,
and insisted on going with them to the police
station. She said that it would be dark soon
and she wanted to get the children home.

An inspector, who looked very important, listened to the policeman's story. 'Show me the gold,' he said.

Cyril put his hands in his pockets – and his face changed. He began to laugh. There was no gold! The children searched their pockets. So did the police. There wasn't a guinea left.

'The sun's set!' said Jane.

'Yes, it has, and it's time I took these children home,' said Martha. 'If you officers have *quite* finished bullying them. You'll be hearing from their father.'

Martha took them home in a carriage, but she gave them a severe talking-to for going into town by themselves. They had to promise never to do it again.

The only guinea which did not disappear was the one they had used to pay for the pony cart. The man made a hole in it, and hung it from his watch chain.

CHAPTER 4

The Lamb

The next wish was an unfortunate accident.

Since meeting the Psammead, the children had had two wishes. Both had left them hungry and in trouble. Wishing for what you wanted was not as easy as it looked. They tried to talk this over during breakfast, but the Lamb was being as difficult as he knew how to be. He tried to get out of the high chair and nearly choked himself. Then he hit Cyril with a spoon and upset the goldfish tank over everyone. It wasn't easy rescuing all the goldfish, and then everyone needed to change into dry clothes.

They were hurrying off at last to the gravel pit, when Martha ran after them. 'Take him with you today!' she said. 'I've got so much to do!'

'Oh, but...' began Anthea.

'No, thanks,' said Robert.

'But he's such a little love!' cried Martha, handing over the Lamb. 'How can you not want him! Anyone would want him, bless him!'

It was worse at the gravel pit. It's impossible to mind a lively baby and dig for a Psammead at the same time. Then the Lamb knocked over their precious bottle of lemonade and Robert lost his temper.

'He's a nuisance!' he cried. 'I wish everyone *did* want him!'

There was a terrible silence. Then the Psammead's furry head popped up. 'Done it!' he said.

'Oh please,' said Jane, 'won't you undo it?'

'Certainly not,' said the Psammead, and buried itself in a flurry of sand.

'We'd better go home,' said Cyril. 'And we'll have to make sure nobody sees the Lamb. Otherwise they'll all want him.'

They walked home gloomily. Anthea tried to hide the Lamb in her coat, but he thought it was a game and kept throwing it off. He had just done this for the third time when a carriage came up behind them.

'Out of the way for her Ladyship,'* shouted the coachman* as he passed.

Then all of a sudden, the carriage stopped in front of them. Out stepped a very beautiful lady.

'What an adorable baby!' she cried. 'I usually can't stand children, but I simply must have this little darling. I'm Lady Chittenden, you know, and I can bring him up like a prince. I shall adopt* him.'

She snatched the baby from Anthea's arms, sprang into the carriage and cried, 'Drive on!'

The children rushed after the carriage and held on. The faster the carriage went, the faster they had to run.

Just as they thought they couldn't keep going any longer, it stopped at a small, stone cottage. Beyond this was an enormously long drive leading to a big grand house that must be Lady Chittenden's.

'Coachman,' she ordered, 'I must speak to the gardener's wife. I shall leave my dear little angel in the back of the coach. Watch him for me.'

Lady Chittenden stepped out to tell the
gardener's wife that she must come to the
big house and look after the Lamb as his new
nanny. In the coach, the coachman turned to
gaze adoringly at the little boy.

The gardener came to see what he was
looking at. 'What a beautiful little lad!' said
the gardener. 'What's he doing in there? Her
ladyship hates children!'

'I won't let her near him,' said the coachman.
'*I'm* keeping him!'

'You're not!' said the gardener. 'He's coming
home with *me*.'

'I saw him first!' said the coachman, and
pushed the gardener out of the way. Then
their coats were off and their fists were up.

The coachman and the gardener fought each other up and down the lane.

'Make them stop!' squealed Jane, as the gardener punched the coachman on the nose.

'I don't think anyone can stop them,' said Cyril, as the coachman knocked the gardener over. 'Let's get the Lamb while we can.'

Anthea glanced over her shoulder. 'She's coming back!' she cried.

Cyril grabbed the Lamb from the seat and together the children ran into the trees. They worked their way deeper into the woodland.

'Everybody *does* want him,' said Cyril. 'We'd better get home quickly.'

'We can't go by the main road,' said Anthea. 'Anybody who sees him will try to take him away.'

So they went home by a long, winding route that took them miles out of their way. Fourteen times they had to hide in the hedge to protect the Lamb from passers-by. One

woman *did* see him, and they had to make a run for it.

At last they got home, tired and hot and fed up. Then Jane pointed out that they couldn't take him into the garden in case anyone passed by the gate and saw him. So they had to spend the rest of a sunny afternoon indoors, keeping him amused.

'And I didn't wish for *this*,' grumbled Robert.

CHAPTER 5

Wings!

The next day was both ordinary and very special because Uncle Richard called.* He took them out, let them choose something from the shop and took them all out to tea. So they hardly even thought about the Psammead.

The day after that, Anthea suggested a wish, and they all thought it was a wonderful idea.

Wings! When it had granted the wish, even the Psammead thought they looked amazing. After a few practice jumps and flaps, they were flying, soaring through the air on wide, soft wings that changed colour in the sunlight.

They swooped, rose and fell, feeling the

wind guiding them and rushing past their faces. Far over the country, they looked down over houses and gardens, woods and rivers, roads and trains. When they were hungry, they helped themselves from fruit trees. But fruit wasn't enough, and it's astonishing how hungry you get when you're flying. They had also flown much further than they had meant to. They settled on a high church tower to talk.

'We can't go to a shop like this,' said Cyril.

'And we can't fly all the way home with nothing to eat or drink,' said Robert firmly.

'Perhaps the vicar of this church will help us,' suggested Anthea. 'He knows all about angels.'

'Only we're not angels,' Jane pointed out. 'And we don't look like them. We're too dirty.'

'I saw a window open at the vicarage,' said Cyril. 'A larder* window. We could fly down to that and...'

'We can't steal food from the vicar!' said Jane.

'I think it's all right if you're starving,' said Cyril.

'If we take food, we pay for it,' said Anthea firmly. 'Let's see how much money we have between us.'

They agreed that half a crown* would be enough to pay for dinner, flew down, and hovered at the larder window. Cyril reached in and handed out food to the rest of them – cold meat, chicken, a loaf of bread and a bottle of soda water. (He felt they should only take what they really needed, so he left the cakes and puddings, which looked delicious.)

They left the money on the windowsill, wrapped in a scribbled note in which Anthea explained that they had only taken the food because they were starving. Then they flew back to the tower.

With no knives and forks and nothing to wipe their fingers on, the picnic was disgustingly messy, but they all felt much better for it. Tired and well fed, they curled up under the warm softness of their wings and fell asleep.

Cold woke them at last. For a few seconds, none of them could work out where they were. Then the truth sank in. The sun had set, and the wings that had kept them warm had disappeared.

'We're stranded!' cried Jane.

'Don't panic,' said Cyril. 'The first thing is to get down from this tower. Then we'll find the way home. There's a door in the tower, we can get down that way.' But when he tried the door, it was locked from the other side.

They were stuck on top of a tower after dark, a long way from home.

'Shout for help,' said Cyril. 'There are lights on at the vicarage, so they're in. Let's hope they don't find out that we took the food. Or we'll be arrested for stealing.'

'You said it wasn't stealing!' said Anthea. 'We paid!'

'They might not see it that way,' said Cyril. 'But we can't stay here all night. Shout!'

They shouted, yelled and screamed. The vicarage door opened.

'Somebody's being murdered in the church!' cried the vicar. 'The lunatic who stole the chicken must be running wild! I must go at once!'

'Not alone!' cried his wife.

So the vicar asked Andrew, the handyman, to go with him. Andrew said that there might be a whole gang up there and they should get more help. The cook's cousin was sent for. His name was Beale, and he was a gamekeeper. So the three of them crept up the tower stairs, with Beale leading the way.

'Who's up there?' he shouted through

the keyhole.

The children were shivering with cold and fear.

'Just us,' said Cyril. 'Please let us out!'

'How many of you?' asked Beale.

'Four,' said Cyril.

'Stand well away from the door,' called Beale.

'We will!' they called.

'They sound like children!' said the vicar. 'Go gently, Beale!'

'Bless me!' said Beale as he heaved the door open. 'You're right, sir! It's just kids!'

The children were all taken to the vicarage. The vicar asked them what they had been doing in the tower and how they got up there. But when Jane burst into tears and flung herself into the arms of the vicar's wife, everybody became very kind.

'It's just a bit of fun that's got out of hand,' whispered Beale to the vicar. 'I reckon somebody put them up to it, and they won't tell.'

'Children,' asked the vicar, 'was anybody else mixed up in this?'

All the children thought of the Psammead.

'Yes,' said Anthea carefully, 'but they didn't mean any harm.'

'Let's say no more about it,' said the vicar. 'Beale, will you take the children home? But they should have something to eat first.'

By the time the carriage was ready for them, the children were having cake and hot drinks and laughing at the vicar's jokes.

Beale took them home and explained to Martha that they hadn't been doing any harm.

In fact, he stayed for a long time talking to
Martha, who wasn't as cross as she might have
been. He came to see Martha a lot after that.

CHAPTER 6

The field of battle

Martha had been very worried by the children staying out so late – in spite of what Beale said about it – and the next day, they weren't allowed out. Robert escaped to ask the Psammead for a wish, but he couldn't think of anything that they'd all like.

'I don't know what to wish for,' he said, sitting by the Psammead in the sunshine. 'It would be much easier if we could have wishes without having to come here. I wish we could. Then one of the others could wish for something and – no, don't!'

It was too late. The Psammead was already

swelling up almost to bursting point.
'Difficult,' it said. 'And that's two wishes.
Off you go, because they've just wished for
something really silly.'

Robert ran all the way to the house – and
stopped suddenly. It wasn't the house at all.
A great castle stood there, with towers and
battlements,* exactly like a castle in a story.
Around it, dotted about, were tents, heavily
armed soldiers, and horses. Weapons clanked
and harnesses* rattled.

'They didn't just wish for a castle!' thought
Robert. 'They've wished for a castle under
siege!* This lot are dangerous and they're
going to attack!'

Two soldiers were coming towards him. He
wanted to run away but he knew he wouldn't
get far, so he stood still and let them take him
by the arms.

'Brave lad!' said one. 'Why art thou here?
Where dwellest thou?'

'What? Oh, you mean, "where do I live",'
said Robert. 'Over there.'

'In the castle!' said one of the soldiers. 'Then come to our leader, Wulfric de Talbot!'*

Robert was marched to the leader and gasped with admiration. Wulfric de Talbot sat on a magnificent warhorse and was dressed in full armour, complete with helmet and sword. He took off his helmet to show a kind face and long straggling hair.

'Child,' he said, 'why art thou on the field of battle?'

'Er – by accident,' said Robert. 'I didn't mean to be here. Neither did you, I mean, thou. Thou aren't quite real.'

'I would fight thee for those words,' said the knight, 'but thou art a child. If this castle does not surrender by sundown, this will be a field of battle. My men are armed and ready to fight to the death. It is no place for you. Go where you will.'

'Thanks!' said Robert and ran back to find the Psammead.

'Not you again!' grumbled the Psammead. 'I've done two wishes today already, and one was extremely difficult.'

'Please, please,' said Robert. 'I wish I were with the others!'

The Psammead swelled up. Robert found himself in the castle.

'Hello!' said Cyril. 'Isn't this fun!'

'Fun!' yelled Robert. 'There are soldiers out there, with swords and lances, bows and arrows – not toys, *real* weapons. And they know how to use them! They're going to attack at sundown – the leader told me! Are there any soldiers here on our side?'

'Haven't a clue,' said Cyril. 'We haven't explored yet.'

The children began looking around their castle. There was a wide moat all around it, the drawbridge was up, and the portcullis* was down. So far, so good. But when they wished for a castle, they hadn't wished for any soldiers to help them defend it.

Crossing the courtyard in the middle, Anthea gasped in horror. The Lamb seemed to be sitting in mid air. Martha was smiling at

him. Anthea dashed to catch the baby.

'Let him alone, miss,' said Martha. 'He's quite happy in his high chair. He's watching me do the ironing.'

'They haven't noticed anything!' whispered Cyril. 'It's because of our wish! They're all in the house as usual, doing the everyday things. And we're in the castle. Only they can't see the castle and we can't see the house, even though it's all in the same place.'

'We can't *feel* the ordinary things, either,' said Anthea. 'I couldn't feel the high chair.'

Robert looked white and worried. 'If we can't *feel* things,' he said, 'can we taste them?

I mean – what about dinner?'

They found out where the dining room was because they saw Martha carrying an invisible tray. They followed her. Luckily, their dining room at home was in the castle's banqueting hall.

'But there's nothing on the tray!' whispered Jane.

'There is,' Anthea whispered back. 'But we can't see it.'

They sat down at the table, glumly watching Martha serve invisible food on to invisible plates. When she had gone they ran their hands along the table. They felt nothing.

'I've got some biscuits in my pockets,' said Cyril. He carefully shared out three broken biscuits between the four of them. They tasted of string and pencil and whatever else had been in Cyril's pocket, but the children were too hungry to mind.

'Hang on,' said Robert. 'How come the dinner's invisible and untouchable – but the biscuits aren't?'

Cyril thought about this. 'I suppose it's because the biscuits were in my pocket, so it's as if they were part of me,' he said.

'Then, if we ate the *dinner*, that would be part of us,' said Robert.

'It's worth a try,' said Cyril. He bent over the table and took a bite, the way a dog eats from a bowl. He looked up with his mouth full, gravy on his nose, and a big smile on his face.

'It works!' he said.

They all tried it. The food could not be seen or touched. But it became real as soon as they bit into it. It was the messiest meal they had ever eaten and when Martha came in she said she'd never seen such a state in all her life. But nobody was hungry any longer.

'Time to get ready for a battle, then!' said Cyril. They climbed to the top of the tower to look down at the army that was laying siege to them. But when they saw the soldiers sharpening their swords and dragging in a tree trunk to use as a battering ram,* they all felt very shaky.

'There are holes in the floor of the gate tower for pouring down boiling lead,'* said Anthea. 'But we don't have any.'

'Quick, let's look in the armoury and see what we *do* have,' said Cyril. 'We'll just have to do our best, that's all. They were all scared by now, but nobody wanted to show it.

There were swords, shields, and bows and arrows in the armoury. But they were meant for full-grown men and much too heavy for them, so they each took a stick. Then they decided to put a pot of water in the guard tower, ready to pour down instead of boiling lead.

'Those soldiers really know what they're doing, don't they?' said Cyril. 'And there are a lot of them.'

'I don't like this wish!' said Jane. 'This isn't fun any more.'

'It never was!' said Robert.

When the water pot was ready, there was nothing to do but wait at the gatehouse window. A trumpet call made their spines shiver.

'Surrender this castle,' demanded the trumpeter, 'or we will put it to fire and sword. Not one man, woman or child shall be spared. Do you surrender?'

'Never!' shouted Robert, and the others joined him, cheering and shouting. Their voices sounded very thin, but banging the sticks against the wall helped.

'It must be nearly sunset,' said Jane.

'Shh!' said Robert.

They heard the clank of chain-mailed feet.

below them. Somebody had got in!

'They've swum the moat!' cried Robert. He dashed to the door and locked it.

'I can hear another one!' said Cyril. 'And listen – somebody's lowering the drawbridge!'

'Quick! The boiling lead!'

Anthea heaved up the pot to tip water on the attackers, her hands shaking. Would sunset never come?

'Dost thou still dare to stand out against us?' called an angry voice.

'Surrender!'

Then the drawbridge was lowered. Jane shrank against Anthea.

The battering ram thudded against the door – but only once. Suddenly, all became silent. The children rushed to the window. The soldiers and their tents had disappeared. The sun had set and the garden was the garden again. The house was just a house.

'At least we didn't get into trouble,' said Anthea. 'It's the first adventure we've had without Martha being cross.'

The door flew open. In walked Martha, her hair and shoulders dripping. 'And just what do you think you're playing at?' she cried. 'Throwing water out of windows? Straight to bed with the lot of you, this minute!'

CHAPTER 7

Lady Chittenden's diamonds

The next morning was full of news. The first
thing was about Martha, who was too happy
to keep a secret. Beale, the gamekeeper who
had rescued them from the church tower,
had asked her to marry him, and she had said
yes. Then there was a letter to tell them that
Granny was better, and Mother was coming
home that day. Father would be home too,
in the evening. The children's whole world
looked happier, and they agreed at once that
they would use the day's wish for Mother.
They were trying to guess what she would like
when Martha came in, full of excitement.

'There's been a burglary at Lady Chittenden's house!' she said. 'Beale's just told me! All her beautiful jewellery's been stolen. All her pearls and tiaras and that! She keeps wailing for her diamonds, and fainting!'

'I didn't like Lady Chittenden,' said Jane when Martha had gone. 'I don't see why she should have all that jewellery. Mother hardly has any. *She* should have all those tarrars and things.'

'Tiaras,' said Cyril.

'Let's put some roses in vases,' said Anthea. 'Then she'll come home and find beautiful flowers in her room.'

'It would be even better,' said Jane dreamily, 'if she came home and found all those terraras and diamonds in her room. I wish she would.'

'Oh no!' cried Anthea and Cyril.

'She *will*, now,' said Robert with a sigh. 'You wished.'

'Sorry,' said Jane.

'Quick,' said Cyril. 'Let's find the Psammead. Ask him very nicely if we can wish our way out of it.'

But that morning, they couldn't find the Psammead. They couldn't find the jewels either, though they searched Mother's room.

'I suppose that's not the way the wish works,' said Robert. 'Mother's the one who will find them.'

'She'll be a receiver of stolen goods,' said Robert. 'You can go to prison for that.'

'Don't!' said Anthea. 'Let's make everything ready for her.'

Filling vases with flowers helped to take their minds from Mother being arrested as a jewel thief. She arrived in the afternoon, was hugged with delight by everyone, and admired the flowers. At last, she took off her coat.

'She's going upstairs!' whispered Anthea, and they all clung to Mother. 'I'll take your coat upstairs, Mother.'

'Come and see the garden!' said Robert.

'I really must have a wash,' Mother insisted.

The children trailed glumly up the stairs behind her. On her dressing table lay a sparkling ring.

'Where did that come from?' she asked.

She became more puzzled when she opened the drawer and found it full of diamond necklaces. When a jewelled tiara tumbled out of the wardrobe, Jane's face crumpled into tears.

'Children,' said Mother firmly, 'do you know anything about this?'

'Not a thing,' said Cyril earnestly. 'But Martha just said that there was a burglary at

Lady Chittenden's house last night. Maybe the burglar hid her jewels here!'

It was a brilliant piece of quick thinking. All the children gave a quiet sigh of relief.

'I can't think why a burglar would leave them here,' said Mother, 'but I'll send for the police.'

'Er – let's wait until this evening!' cried Robert.

'Nonsense!' she said, and called for Martha. 'Martha, has anyone been in my room while I've been away?'

Martha burst into tears. 'No,' she said. 'At least, Beale – that's my young man. I was about to tell you about him. He helped me clean the windows this morning. I did the inside and he did the outside. But he wasn't in here.'

'Were you with him all the time?' asked Mother.

'Not quite all the time,' admitted poor Martha.

'Thank you, Martha,' said Mother, very quietly and gravely. 'You may go.'

Martha left the room in tears. The thought of what was about to happen made the children feel ill. Mother would tell the police that Beale had been at the house. Then he would be accused of stealing Lady Chittenden's jewels.

'It wasn't Beale!' sobbed Jane, clinging to Mother. 'He's lovely, he's kind – it wasn't him!'

'I must go to the police at once,' said Mother. 'I shall leave this room locked. Boys, stay here, and let nobody in.'

'Now Beale will be arrested as a jewel thief,' muttered Cyril after she'd gone. 'Or, if the police arrive after sunset, they'll arrest Mother for wasting police time. However you look at it, it's a ghastly mess.'

'We'll try again to find the Psammcad,' said Anthea. 'It's a hot day. He might have come out to get the sun on his whisker.'

'He won't give us more wishes, though,' said Jane. 'I think he hates it.'

Anthea jumped to her feet. 'One last chance,' she said. 'Come with me, Jane!'

They ran to the gravel pit and found the Psammead sunning itself. When it saw them it tried to hide. But Anthea caught it and held it fast.

'Not *more* wishes!' protested the Psammead.

'Dearest, lovely Psammead,' soothed Anthea, 'do you hate giving wishes?'

'You can't imagine how much!' it wailed. 'I'm always afraid that I'll hurt myself. I'd give you all the wishes you want today, I'd go on until I almost burst, if I knew I'd never have to give wishes again!' Its voice became very high and tearful. 'One day I *will* burst!'

'Poor Psammead,' said Anthea. 'We need your help now. But if you can grant us all our wishes today, we promise never to ask for anything else.'

'Go on, then,' said the Psammead.

'I wish that the jewels weren't stolen at all,' said Anthea.

The Psammead swelled up. 'Done,' it said.

'And that Mother doesn't get to the police,' said Anthea.

'Done,' said the Psammead after an effort.

'And that she and Martha forget all about it,' said Anthea.

'Done,' said the Psammead at last, weakly. 'Will you wish something for me?'

'Can't you grant wishes for yourself?' asked Anthea in surprise.

'Of course not,' it said. 'Will you wish that none of you will ever be able to tell about me? I so want to be left alone.'

Anthea wished it. 'Now have a lovely rest,' she said. 'I hope we meet again one day.'

'Is that a wish?' it asked.

'Yes, please,' they said.

The Psammead blew itself out. Then, for the last time, it buried itself in the sand.

At home, Anthea and Jane had only just told the boys what they'd done when Mother arrived, hot and tired.

'I was on the way to town,' she said, 'and the cart overturned! I've had to walk back. I'd love a cup of tea!'

Martha was making the tea when Beale

arrived. 'You know I said there was a burglary at the Chittenden place?' said Beale. 'It wasn't a burglary at all! Lord Chittenden had sent the jewellery away to be cleaned, and her ladyship didn't know. So all's well.'

'Yes,' said Anthea. 'All's well.'

'Do you think we'll ever see the Psammead again?' said Jane at bedtime.

'I'm sure we will,' said Anthea. 'His magic always works.'

'But it never works how we think it will, does it?' said Robert. 'So we'll see him just when we don't expect it.'

And he was right. But that's another story.

E Nesbit
(born 1858, died 1924)

Edith Nesbit was born in England but spent her childhood in France and Germany and later moved to Kent. She published her books under the name E Nesbit because she did not want people to know if she was a man or a woman. She thought boys might not want to read her books if they knew she was a female author.

Nesbit was quite unusual for her time. She was very outspoken and had strong views about how the country should be run. She and her husband set up a political group. She wrote poems and for political newspapers and magazines. She also wrote plays, novels and ghost stories.

Nesbit's children's books were mostly about family life. Her most famous book is *The Railway Children*, which has been made into several films and television series. Sometimes the family gets mixed up in magic, as in this book *Five Children and It*.

Best known works
Books
The Railway Children
The Story of the Treasure Seekers

Sequels to *Five Children and it*
The Phonenix and the Carpet
The Story of the Amulet

Margaret McAllister

Margaret has spent most of her life in Northumberland but now lives in Yorkshire. She is married to a clergyman and has three grown-up children. She trained to teach English, but ended up working in an office, then teaching dance and drama in an Arts Centre. She did all sorts of jobs before writing full time – teaching adult education, home tuition, cleaning a church, washing up in a tearoom, and sometimes several of those at once.

Margaret loved stories and storytelling – she was making up stories in her head before she was old enough to write them down. Over the last ten years Margaret has written several TreeTops books, the three Mistmantle Chronicles featuring Urchin the squirrel, and a teenage novel, *High Crag Linn* set in the fifteenth century.

About E Nesbit, Margaret says, 'I've enjoyed her books ever since a teacher at junior school read *The Treasure Seekers* to the class. The children in her books may have very different lives from ours – no electrical gadgets, no cars and some very uncomfortable clothes! – but they have real personalities that spring into life. They squabble a bit, but they really do look after each other. Their adventures are exciting, but they always end up in a muddle and have to get themselves out of it.'

Notes about this book

Five Children and It was published in 1902, a year after the death of Queen Victoria. This was a time when most people still travelled by horse-drawn vehicles, or by train. There were very few cars.

The children in this book are from a family that is quite well off. They have their own horse and carriage, and they can afford to rent a large house in the countryside for the summer holidays that has two servants – a cook and a maid – to look after them.

Five Children and It was made into a BBC series in 1991 and into a film in 2004. The adventures of the children continue in *The Phoenix and the Carpet* and *The Story of the Amulet*.

Page 6

* **chalk quarry** A large pit in the ground that has been dug to extract chalk – used in the building industry (and on blackboards!)

* **gravel pit** A large pit in the ground that has been dug to extract gravel – used in building and road works. Gravel is made up of little pieces of stones that have been worn smooth in rivers. The stones are usually found mixed with sand, so when the gravel is taken away the area is left as a sandy pit.

Page 11

* **Psammead** This is the 'It' character – a sand-fairy invented by Nesbit for this book. She made up the name using the Ancient Greek word for 'sand'. This word starts with the Greek letter 'Psi' (which sounds like 'sigh').

Page 12
***megatherium** A large animal that lived about 2 million to 8000 years ago. They were covered in fur, were as big as elephants and ate plants.

Page 13
***turned to stone** This is a very old idea that is used in many myths and fairy tales. In the book *The Hobbit,* trolls turn to stone when the sun comes up.

Page 28
***spade guineas** A guinea is an old British gold coin that was worth 21 shillings or £1.05. A spade guinea was a special type of guinea coin made in the time of King George III with a spade-shaped shield on it.

Page 30
***tuppence** Means 'two pence'. The word 'tuppence' was used especially before new coins were introduced in Britain in 1971. Some people still talk about 2p coins as 'tuppenny pieces'.

Page 37
***her Ladyship** A polite way of talking about someone who is a lady.
***coachman** Someone who drives a carriage.
***adopt** To take someone into your family and treat them as your own child.

Page 45
***called** To call on someone means to visit them.

Page 46
***larder** A cupboard or small room used for storing food.

Page 47
* **half a crown** An old British coin that was worth just over 10p.

Page 55
* **battlements** The top of a castle wall which usually has notches from which arrows can be shot.
* **harnesses** Leather straps with buckles placed over a horse's head and neck to control it.
* **siege** When one army surrounds a town or castle and stays there until the army or people inside run out of food and water and surrender.

Page 57
* **Wulfric de Talbot** A medieval lord. English lords often had French surnames because in 1066 a French man, William the Conqueror, became king of England.

Page 58
* **portcullis** A gate or door at a castle entrance that could quickly be dropped down to prevent people entering.

Page 61
* **battering ram** A heavy pole used to break through the walls and gateways of a town or castle.

Page 62
* **pouring down boiling lead** Medieval castles were built with many ways to protect the people inside from attack. One way was to have a hole from which boiling water or hot sand could be poured on to anyone trying to break in. Some people believe boiling lead was also used this way, although it is unlikely because lead was so expensive.